PRIMATE FOX
Late Poems (2010–2011)

Hugh Fox

MadHat Press
Asheville, North Carolina

MadHat Press
MadHat Incorporated
PO Box 8364, Asheville, NC 28814

Copyright © 2010-2012 Hugh Fox
All rights reserved

The Library of Congress has assigned
this edition a Control Number of
2012952885

ISBN 978-0-9885490-1-2 (paperback)

Text by Hugh Fox
Cover painting by Tristan Daniel Tanta and Gene Tanta
Book and cover design by MadHat Press and Jonathan Penton

www.madhat-press.com

CONTENTS

I.
NIGHT-WATCHMAN-NESS

Re-Inspiriting	9
Blu-Ray Rerun	10
Back Home	11
The Time Of	12
In Between	13
Re-In-Psyche-Action	14
Primate Fox	15
To Look / *Olhar*	16
All of a Sudden	17
Christmas(ing)	18
Iguatemi / *Iguatemi*	19
Everything	21
Loving	22
Alternatives	23
From Now	24
Now	25
The Eternal	26
Wherevers	28
The Confessional Diary of Bone Boning	29
Class War	30
The Seconds	31
What Do I?	32
Since	33
Death-Sentence	34
Re-Dying	35
Walking Into	36
Going Back	37
Turning Into	38
Everyday Shalom	39

II.
HARVESTING OUR DOING-NESS

Versus	43
Getting Inside	44
Turning	45
Every	46
Word Garden	47
The Closer	48
Toy Storing	49
Our Afternoon Drive	50
Seeing It	51
Last Visit	52
Once Again	54
Cherimoya	55
Wipe Up	56
Mid	57
Listening	58
Time To …	59
My Last Waltz	61
Sliding	62
Fragmentos	63
Rebirthing Without Having to Die	67
Getting Confused	68
Survival	69
Back Again	70
Turning Off	71
Paranes	72
Zenning	73
La Paix / Peace	74
Brusquement / Suddenly	76

Primate Fox

I.

NIGHT-WATCHMAN-NESS

Re-Inspiriting

The same (incarnation/CARNE), but *espiritu* dying and reborn every day now, drifting through my people-kings speared pasts wrapped in beowulfian

capes looking for my Celtic to-comes, then passing through nun-life knees, knees, knees, and "Bless me Father, for I have …," been forgiven, re-fiddling on the

roof again every Shabbat as my night-mind re-creates the astrological-theosophical galleries of tigereyes, lobster claws, zebra stripes, my wives; dead-again,

born-again faces that spin back and forth between mother-son adoration and an androgynous mountain-top-ness long ago crucified and tombed.

Hugh Fox

BLU-RAY RERUN

Eye-nose-and-mouth-less grey sky, "The
eleven-inch snowfalls in Montana …," even with
the screen talking back wanting to time-travel
back to potato-cook time in the side yard next
to our apartment building, drives out to Henry
the Eighth's Tudorville, envying the houses, yards,
cars, "Some day …," that came and went and
the next generation's ballet-and-soccer-legs dance/lance
through the door out into "See ya soon" estate-planned
hopefulness.

Back Home

Back home economically
these days, 1930s Chicago,
"Man, look at that house, those
pillars out in front, I don't know if
they really go with the brick, but …,"
weekend drives into Big Money
suburbs like Oak Park, which looked
like Hollywood, and then back to the
far South Side, all the peasants like
my grandma, my pa—an M.D., but he
could just as well have been a construction
worker, home-calls but no home, crappy
apartment in a crappy apartment building,
me working summer digging ditches,
delivering mail, we could just as well have
still been back in Czechville, on the Irish
coast, like I tell my Brazilian brother-in-
law every weekend, "You'd be better off
in Brazil," he smiles back, "This week …
but you never know."

Hugh Fox

The Time Of

Suddenly all the divorce-court
property disputes, "How could you
have …? " "Not interested!"
"I happen to have found a
new …," gone, all in our late
seventies, me looking like a
nineteenth-century tweeded
Londoner again, just resurrected
from the grave, my two ex-
and-one-still-married wives
looking like *Pride and Prejudice*,
Ozark Queens, my own Grandma
Mary with her long skirts and flat
black shoes, long white perfectly
flat-out combed hair, a little coffee
at Big Apple Bagel or "Let's try
The Tuba Gallery for dinner, I
love their salads," a Verdehr (violin),
Votapek (piano) concert, or just
the perfect back-porch time, the
main thing the years of selves
shared, rejected, now starving for.

In Between

Between the first *WAH*
and the last *RRRF*,
between the first into-the-gorge
plunge and the final carcinogenic
orchiectomy, between the first
Steinway creation chords and
Satie-ian non-melodies and
banging the key-cover on
your frozen claws, between
the first poem-vision sliding
down the Wordsworthian hills
to the final cybernetic listening
to the muse-voices crackling
into your amplified ears,
those legs, those veins,
those mammalian feeders,
wheelchair down the
last corridor to make a
reservation on the right
hill in the WE HOPE
wilderness
sleepyard.

Hugh Fox

Re-In-Psyche-Action

No matter how much the bone-mites have decimated
you, you're still there/here sauerkrauting
and sausaging it, I don't want your
pure ghost with me for
all eternity, but back in Prague
side-streeting it through Mala Strana
forever, back to forty-five and me
a sumptuous grandsonish five.

Primate Fox

Days in Chicago-Detroit-Brooklyn,
bangitty-bang-bang hammers
and liquid concrete trucks,
pouring out the roads, building
the red-brick apartment houses,
all the late 1930s and 40s,
my MD father got me a ditch-
digging (new streets) job for
two summers, me and all the
Irishmen, Italians, Sicilians,
a little beer, wine ... and go back
to No Job now, a house a day
coming down in Flint-Detroit,
Chicago ... a murder a day,
usually break-ins, thinking
maybe I ought to get a dog,
a gun, sleep during the day,
retired, sludging into Rest
in Night-Watchman-ness.

Hugh Fox

To Look

The first look, they're savage seductresses, twenty, twenty-five, degrees in commercial economy or doctors, pathologists, specialists in cybernetics ... you know, animal hair but very carefully taken care of, the legs, marble ankles turned into flesh, hands that reach out for me like a white bear grabbing walruses, another look and there's a hundred and twenty more, still faces, bodies, spirits whispering "Now, no one but you."

Olhar

O *primeiro olhar, é uma sedutora selvagem,*
títulos em economia
comercial ou médicos, patologistas,
especialistas na cibernética... você sabe,
o cabelo animalesco mas bem ciudado,
as pernas, tornozelos de marmore transformadas em
carne, mãos que me procuram como um
urso branco que agarra morsas,
um outro olhar e há cento e vinte mais,
rostos imóveis, corpos, espiritos sussurrando
"Agora, mais ninguem só voce."

All of a Sudden

I throw the news out on to my Contact List,
120 contacts, some of them in the morgue
for years, "My oncologist just told me that
I've got a maximum of 2 years to live with
my prostate cancer, no known cures to make
me last longer …," and all of a sudden … there's
Fanny Winward on Long Island, kind of a combo
of Dietrich and Coccinelle, 20 years of silence
since I wrote a book in which I told the truth-
truth-truth about her when the sun went down
and her aged husband went to sleep, now pictures
of aging but still ecstatic her, her kids, grandkids,
a few poems about lilacs and legs, sundown,
funup, then Rich Dunthrope out in San Francisco,
10 films based on his novels, old, bored, kind
of semi-paralyzed, couple of strokes, "So fight
back, chemo-everythings, look at me, the
hospital's a battlefield," my long-lost-pissed-off
daughter Gabrielle in Tokyo (teaching English),
mad since I walked out on her Japanese mother
20 years ago, "Come over here, Dad, you never
know what they might come up with!," all the
old poets, ex-lovers, friends from grammar
school, high school, college, teaching-mates
at the forty colleges I taught at, my alone-
time house suddenly cyberneticized into
the Old Days in Berkeley, Brooklyn, Cambridge,
Beat-Wild-Rebel-Hippy-Drippy-Divine Time
filling the emptiness with Time Reborn.

Hugh Fox

CHRISTMAS(ING)

Christmas and Chanuka blasting
Polonaise from Rimsky-Korsakov's
Christmas Eve Suite into the BBC's
Slaughter-Evening News, vegan
deer on the side of the road waiting
to be shot, does grass feel pain/loss?
fifty, sixty, a hundred years, what
percentage aging? what percentage
Delibesian-Coppélia *ailes de pigeon,
ballotté, chaînés, ciseaux, joyeuse* dying?

bring them all back, Christmas-Chanukah
dinner every night (car-break-ins during
services), me remembering Christmases
along the Thames. Next to Notre Dame,
letting beliefs in afterlives rain-cover
all the year-second before ascending
winged "death."

Primate Fox

IGUATEMI

A man we don't know appears, we're
having coffee and *casadinhos* (chocolate with
solid sweet milk), in front of Ponto Frio (a
TV store) and Cavalira (fine, fine, fine men's
clothes), he stops "Everything OK?" "Everything
OK," "And you are?" "Jesus Christ," looking at his
hands, no scars, "No scars on the hands?," "everything
healed thousands of years ago … and time doesn't
count for me!" "And for us?" The mute voice
fills the whole mall, "My father, me and my brother
created everything, but you people improved everything
so much, I never saw such luxury, me and the Garden
of Eden next to your computerized world, neither I
or my father or my phantom brother ever made anything
so miraculous, and the food here, I'm going to
reincarnate myself in order to eat the sweets here, and
it's positively time to marry a woman with those sword
legs, cow breasts, eyes of black holes among the stars …
begin again, but everything based on the reality here …,"
and suddenly he throws us a kiss and disappears, a
moment on the TV screen (Samsung) in the window
          of Ponto Frio

                  and

        God   bye

Hugh Fox

IGUATEMI

Um senhor que não conhecemos aparece, nós
tomando café e casadinho (chocolate e
doce de leite sólido) em frente ao Ponto Frio (loja de eletrodomesticos)
e Cavalira (moda masculina fina, fina,
fina) ele para, "Tudo bem?," "Tudo bem."
"Voce é...?," "Jesus Cristo," olhando a suas
mãos, nada de cicatrizes, "não há cicatrizes em suas mãos?
"Tudo curado fazem milhares de
anos ... e o tempo não conta para mim! "E para nós?,"
a voz muda enche o shopping inteiro, "Meu
pai, eu e o meu irmão criamos tudo, mas vocês
melhoram isso tudo muito, nunca vi tanto luxo, eu e o
Jardim do Éden ao lado de seu mundo informatizado,
nem eu, meu pai ou o meu irmão fantasma fizemos nada tão
milagroso, e a comida daqui, eu vou reencarnar-me para comer os doces aqui, e é
positivamente a hora de me casar com uma mulher com aquelas pernas de espada,
peitos de vaca, olhos de buracos negros entre as estrelas ... começar não de novo mas
tudo construido sobre a realidade daqui...," de
repente nos manda um beijo e desaparece, um
momento na tela da televisão (Samsung) na janela
          do Ponto Frio

               e

     A   Deus

Primate Fox

Everything

As I move rather rapidly into Death, Reality
runs into … let's call it Magic … getting up and
breakfasting looking out at the coniferous needle-
scale-leaved backyard hills, three Magic deer passing
down to the river, Mom, Dad and Fawn, a thousand
birds getting ready to, what, flee the descending-
upending cold, grey-skies turning into cloud-island
brightness, where did I come from, where am I going,
how did the billion-ness of Space ever begin, created
out of Nothingness to Everything-ness, all my astro-
physicist friends and their theory-equations leading back
beyond magic to what can only be supernatural
beginnings, never really
beginning and never really
                                        closing down

Hugh Fox

LOVING

Santa Catarina Island, Brazilian summer at Lourdes'
home on the beach, fifty steps and you're in the water,
a few degrees below body temperature so you become
the sea and the sea becomes you. / *E os tubarãos...?* /
What about the sharks and...? I used to ask thirty years ago
when I first married Lourdes' sister, Bernadete, after watching
the boats down the coast bring in their spear-nosed
scalpel-toothed catch, *Nâo tem ...* / *There aren't any ...* why not?
and then dinner on the hill overlooking the sea, Lourdes
supposedly dying of pancreatic cancer, but they keep
operating, bio-chemical her and at sixty-four she still
looks twenty-four, wind, here comes the wind, here come
the storms, but her concrete-block house is built for it,
open all the windows, let it come in ... brother Paulo takes
me over to his house and for the first time in thirty years
I swimsuit into his perfect pool, lying back on a float-
bed, the trees in just the right place to block the afternoon
sun, seventy-eight but slowly becoming ten again,
in Miami for our family summer, not a Fox at all, but a koi
fish, measuring time in centuries, not in days, months,
                      mini-years.

Primate Fox

Alternatives

Feet that never antique out
how many where
and a life of thistles or pass the
sun-steaks

Hugh Fox

From Now

A thousand years from now,
records, remembrances,
a billion astral memories
remembering this screen
and the *papagayo* birds out in
the forest getting used to me.

Primate Fox

Now

And I've just gotten the
final judgment from the
cancer-jury and I can't believe
her taking me around to
perfect-napkin places with
her babies, as if I were one
of them instead of her
        creator.

Hugh Fox

The Eternal

The eternal (deer, turkeys, cranes as we slide by
wilderness and empty corn and soy fields during
daily immersion-in-reality drives, phoning
Alexander in Cambridge, tenth grandson birthday,
"Thanks for the check, and I want to come to
visit over the Christmas-holidays," my getting
the tapioca and papaya ready, engulfed in a few
tablespoons of unpourable titillating Bavarian
honey, the right temperature, bed, bedclothes
and dreaming I'm on stage again (age ten) at the
Opera House in Chicago in the children's chorus
in Carmen, the visiting-travelling Met, Gladys
Swarthout as Carmen, the first snows, the first
spring rains, something mysteriously huge on
the late-fall roof last night, that vanished when
I went outside and started growling at two
a.m., getting totally involved with THE COLOR
PURPLE and the new Schubertian-Debussyian
work by the undergrad students in the Michigan
State University music college, going down to
the beach from my wife's sister's house in
Florianopolis, Brazil, walking out into the ocean
up to my neck, the water about two degrees
colder than my body, just goodnights
and good mornings, my thirty-year-old son
living downstairs saying goodnight,
"I love you," "Me too ...," going to
marry a Thai lawyer beauty, my own
surgeries successful ... for the time being ...,

Primate Fox

the pre-Columbian, Peruvian, Chilean,
Bolivian, South-Dakota relic-covered walls
of my life …) versus …

at 87 every time we pass a cemetery, reading
as many names as I can,

        feeling ….

Hugh Fox

WHEREVERS

There's aging Hari, half-close your eyes and she's fifty (instead of eighty-five), not that it makes any difference, still all smiling hands that make love to keyboards, and then a call, when I get home, from cousin Jack Fewkes in Chicago, "So how's the chemotherapy going? Thinking about you 67.5% of the time...," the old Chicago days never even fractionally leaving me, as if I were some sort of magnoplasmic, timeless creature existing everywhere in all-time that remains timeless, Los Angeles and Bukowski, Buenos Aires and Anita Torres and the rest of the writer gang, New York and all the faces at Benny's deli, Somerville and Gloria Mindock crossing her legs, coffee and mishmash at *Au Bon Pain*, remember the idea I had fifty years ago of creating a retirement Place for all us writers of the '60s and '70s, Richard Morris, Doug Blazek, Dick Higgens, Glenna Luschei, Lynne Savitt, out somewhere on the Northern California hills not far from Fulton's place, my God, all the faces, braces, tongues, eyes, looking, listening, absorbing and then re-creating in words, Lima, Florianopolis, Brazil ... how many wherevers I can still walk into and walk into *abraços*-hugs, kisses, word-crownings, as if I'd never left and gone elsewhere, and, honestly,
                              I never have.

The Confessional Diary of Bone Boning

A week of urine blood, my urologist-oncologist
gives me three different kinds of antibiotics
that collectively turn my nights into Andean
hallucinogenic-mares, last night they were all
there, at first unidentifiable skeletons sitting
around the dining room table chewing on bird
and snake bones, "Our favorites," one old, squat,
thick-bone explains, "You'll find out," trying to figure
out who it/(she?) is, slowly beginning to recognize
them all, old Czech-Jew grandma, and there's tall
MD professional Dad and delicate as sparrow-bones
Mom, Brother Jim, killed in Korea, still all avid and
intense, even with the bones, and wife number 1,
Aviva, killed in an Andean rock-slide at Tiawanaku
when we were on one of our trips looking for God,
the others slowly coming back into recognizableness,
Mr. San Francisco Richard Morris, writing a poem
between bone-bites ... looking at my own hand as
I reach down for a delicacy bone, Richard reading
my bone-brain, "Don't worry it won't be long before
you recognize us all ... including the ones ..."
which I fill in/complete "yet to arrive."

Hugh Fox

CLASS WAR

The only class war growing up in '30s Chicago
was either make it UP or live with DOWN, my
Jewish-Czech grandmother who *could* write, but
very thought-out, slow, carefully forming the letters,
my streetcar-conductor grandfather who died when I
was about three, and I still remember him on his
deathbed, "Bring him closer, I want to give him a
hug," a hug, then the next day the heart stopped,
my MD father and secretary mother always pushing,
pushing me into Medicine after a childhood soaked in The
Arts, always visiting uncles and cousins in the Outback
parts of Chicago, Christmases and Easters, holi-
holy-days, always driving out to rich suburbs like
Oak Park, looking at mansions, IF, IF, IF ... but we
never made it out of the apartment until they retired
to Sun City, California, a great house facing the
desert ... and then died ... a black Nanny when I
was growing up, always loving the blacks and Chinese/
Chinese food, Czech, German, Spanish, always feeling
I was in some sort of United Nations the whole time
I was growing up, Irish nuns, Irish Christian Brothers,
BLESS ME FATHER FOR I HAVE ... my best pal
a black genius, Thomas Simmons, who died this year
at 77, my age, a Harvard law professor most of his life,
married to a Brazilian MD, a week from going down
to Brazil to visit my wife's sister dying from pancreatic
cancer ... never "class" as such ... just Those Who Love
and Those Who Don't (love/accept).

The Seconds

Second sun, second re-cloud, the wind into
my conifers, "You've had it for ten
years, but it seems to be accelerating," my
night-head gothicking back to the year Begin
but never making it.

Hugh Fox

What Do I?

What do I give a crap about your
fancy French country mansions
and your Doctor of Musical Performances,
I can't even believe how many Russians,
Armenians, Chinese, Brazilian, Englishers
are around here, an old Chicago street,
me going to the Chopin and Schumann festivals,
married to a Brazilian MD, retired after teaching
English literature for fifty years, when all I ever
really felt/feel comfortable with were/are the
Chicago, Brooklyn, whore-area bars in Paris,
now, "You've got maybe a year, a year and a half…,"
I'm supposed to believe in heaven and all that, but just believe
in graves, eighty-five years of women, liquor,
lots of criticism published, travel-grants, you
name it, Bukowski's best pal, my best autobiography
named *Way, Way off the Road* to echo
Kerouac's *On the Road*, wishing there was an
after-death L.A.-San Francisco out there waiting
for me, to just keep doing our thing forever, and
that's what I mean.

SINCE

When she first died I thought that was
(button-off) IT, but every night when my
pills finally bring me in, she's there again,
les jambes / the legs and sarcasm about "Olds"
("One more story about a random
shooting in Chicago and …,"), but before
dawn trickles through the slits around the
drapes, her hands begin Rachmaninoff
the stringless keyboard, and at least I
get the sound of fake ivory against fake
Dominus Vobiscum wood.

Hugh Fox

Death-Sentence

Seeing it all differently now,
the Samoan sweet-orange chicken
balls, I eat a few instead of the whole
pile, the feeder in me mostly gone, the
same with my morning cinnamon-oat squares
and even my nightly vermouth, my angry
guts telling me all day "Eat more, we're
frustrated, need exercise," and when night comes
Giselle-Carmen-Coco-Chanel drifts down to her
bedroom away from ten-years-ago-orchiectomied
me looking at the old-time pictures in my
half-frozen bedroom, remembering Gretta in
Florence, Eva in Paris, Chicago, Los Angeles,
Brooklyn, ancient, pre-sound films, fill in
the blanks that daily-nightly become more blank
as they keep talking about my
      last (possible)
       surgery.

Re-Dying

Re-dying again, the Anglo-Saxons coming
in at almost-dawn night as the blood
keeps pissing out, 'When that April with
its sweet showers…,' coming again, wondering
how the Koran-ics and Torah-ics can still be
territorializing as the planet gets more emptied out
daily and everything depends on weight to
keep us where we are, out in the country
passing a just-built old-stone mansion with
a huge driveway, kids' wagons, mom and
three kids, wanting to surround her with
protective shields, like yesterday this
skinny old beauty out alone running down
my favorite dirt-nowhere road, no one (hopefully)
around but observers US, as we escape into
at times untouched forests, rivers, hillscapes for
a couple hours away from the microscopes and
computer screens.

Hugh Fox

WALKING INTO

All of a sudden
the into-the-kitchen walk is over a
Scottish hill into sheep-filled grass lands,
and I lift up the vermouth bottle and
je suis de nouveau chez moi
aber wo?,
walking into the party worlds of
Renoir and Bizet, Chicago never
was really Chicago but a blitzed
throwdown from the sky of fragmented,
torn-up skitterings of all-world history,
in nomine patri et filii ... Melech Ha'olam,
Fathers, Sons, Heaven Kings, unbelieving
but still talking to Hercules/Jesus every night
c. 4 a.m., Mom's ghost an hour into dawn,
the walls still Louvre-Art Institute
talking *'C'est temps de commencer,'*
ninety-one plus....? And then
Kon-Tiki-Viracocha, back to Tiawanaku,
Bolivia, where it all re-begins....

Going Back

Ingesting Jesus, putting a sacred
veil across the whole day, always
the commandments in mind, in spite
of wars, gangs, crookedness spinning
around like schools of sardines
and the fact that we WERE sharks
under our THOU SHALTS and SHALT
NOTS, never imagining breaking into
a suburban house and killing Ms.
Making It, or driving by kids out
playing on the lawn and massacring
them for the WHY-NOT? of it all,
crucifixions and resurrections replaced
by laptop omniscience, disbelieving in
Sinais and the Seas of Galilee, as
everything gets diabolically outsourced
into other realities that have nothing,
to do with We-ness, Do-ness,
Harvesting-Our-Doing-ness.

Hugh Fox

Turning Into

Turning into impressive rain for
a few drizzling moments as
the state warning system comes on
'For Nirgendwo/Nowhere County, a heavy rain
is on the way that may cause severe
damage because of high winds …,'
re-shimmering everything, except
for the ferns which have already wintered
into black-brown, you'd think we drops
were diabolic, everyone turned inward,
off, close them windows, (wo)man!, five
Romeo-and-Juliet minutes and then the
everywhere grey drifts back into sunset
red-orange cloud-dithering games that
slowly sunset into desert cyberneticism.

Everyday Shalom

When the gang comes from Cambridge, Kansas City,
Ann Arbor, Brazil, the Moon, the grandkid brothers and sisters
I never had, and around Margey's smiley-eyes ("I just walked out
on him, he hadn't really talk-talked-relaxed with me for about two
frigid introverted Parisian years.") all kinds of spider-web wrinkles,
Alexander a lot like old-times back fifty year juggler-jongleur
me, can't just sit still and face the sunless snow but "Jack the
Ripper! Only after it's ripped…?," stuck on old Peter Lorre and
Orson Welles films, their Cambridge apartment a kind of museum-
archive of old beyond-horror films, and then Rebecca-Rivka looking
like Swan Like, never a smile-stop, my cousin George from Chicago,
looking like a hippo-squirrel looking for a five-thousand year-oak
that will support his climbing ("Retired into mainly waiting to die
now, although my doctor's optimistic about survival … I wish I could
go back and get Sitting Bull off his ass … time to territory it with
no fooling around!"), former wives Nona and Lucia gobbling down
the chicken and ham like they'd just come out of a Neanderthal
starvation cave, Marcella full of jewels and scarves, looking more
like twenty than fifty-three, "I want you to be around, Dad, around,
around, around, but not too round …," trying to sleep afterwards,
sit-down, roll-over pains that never stop, remembering my
oncologist-urologist, "Cancer's like an explorer. Columbus, the
first trip to the New/Old World, 'Where do I go next?'," no sleep
but the next day the eyes are still there and the rain whispers
"Spring…hope you'll be around to sprinkle on," my eyes and tongue
hanging on to the forest backyard and Santa cookies as long
as they (*liebe, liebe, geliebte/*
love, love, beloved)
                         können/ can.

II.

HARVESTING OUR DOING-NESS

Versus

Blunt stone casements and Hi-Def days
that just as well could have been turned
off year-long Wednesdays and beer-out
slug-out Saturdays sliding into jingle
dreamlands that never come....
    Versus
    Allegro
wallless denominationless ecstatically-plussed
    Now-Days
just like back in Berkeley in 1958

Hugh Fox

Getting Inside

Getting inside the jocular flute slides
and sun-through-the-leaves viola skitters
and cello-violin conversations ("Leave the
way I am, he's the echo, not me!") of Mozart's
Flute Quartet #1, state of the union, brain
shattering, digging out (or death-down) gone
until the rondo takes its last breath.

Turning

Mozart's Flute Quartet #1

Turning sound into just the
right sack-flow silk skirts and
legs, the right sherry, sun on the
invasion hills sanctified for a
thousand years now

                wheat

             thistles

   God

              grasses

                  maple sugarings

Hugh Fox

EVERY

Every water-sip, chocolate-coated raisin
Xanax,
entrance into shoes and suspenders
pillow toss-around,
chemotherapeutic pill,
pulling on of socks,
getting that first crap out
in the morning,
twenty good-night kisses before
sleep-try time,
last words on the last night,
drifting into nowhere

as much ritual as the blessing of
wines,
vines,
god-births.

Words

Remembering back to obsessive Fox back
when I was in high school, everyone else
out-base-and-footballing, me at home
in my cubbyhole bedroom in our apartment
on the far South Side (Chatham) in Chicago,
reading all of Aldous Huxley's and James Joyce's
fiction, St. Augustine's Confessions, Jorge Luis
Borges (in Spanish) … when I'd find a word I didn't
know, keeping notebooks, writing them down, then
the dictionary, let's try Hemingway and T.S.
Eliot, Ezra Pound … brain-notebook … writing sixty
years later, going into my usual word-trances and
here they come again … where did THAT come from,
or, or, or …. memory gone for everything else, but
the word garden somehow still in bloom.

Hugh Fox

THE CLOSER

The closer I get to nowhere, the more they come back,
virginal Joannie Boyle, ten years before she began thirteen
kidding , Dolores still plays Liszt like Arthur Rubenstein before
she ever even thought about law school, Joe and me
Saturdays talking about Hemingway and Aldous Huxley,
Jorge Luis Borges, Pablo Neruda, before he'd ever had any
uniform on, Lake Michigan and The Art Institute, always
another pair of nutcracker ballet legs and Romeo / Juliet
with Chicagoan beyond-pro intensity, loving the snow,
rain, sun, running along the coasting, the first trip to Florence and
meeting Gretta in front of the Mona Lisa, pass the
Vermouth and the (*"Ich kann ... aber ist schwer"*)
language-learning games, all the
infinities coming back as I slowly sink into my final (not
entirely—internet—alone) personal infinity.

Toy Storing

I.

Huge antique toy store with Beatrice (2)
and Alex (42), getting into the doll section,
and the hundreds of eyes staring at me
whispering "More, you should have had
more of us ... while you still could...."

    II.

    Toy store back through tiger-lion-
    kangaroo-polar bear hypnotic Dresden-ish
    doll baby eyes into wordless other-customer-less
     ("Wendy Lawton's Little Women Revisted
    Set, $3,980") time, which is the only time
    I really want to return to.

III.

The world's fanciest toy store, back to
(Made in China) Victorian doll-time,
the old wasted-out owner talking to a pal
near the front door, "The drain-spouts have
to be cleaned out, the front stairs are on the
way out, I'm on the way out," Alice in Wonderland
tea sets, $32.00 tea pot, "Designed in England,
Made in China."

Hugh Fox

OUR AFTERNOON DRIVE

"Country" just a few minutes away, through the corn, wheat, soybean fields, then a patch of dark, heavy forest, the old gods crowding around me, cow-gods, tree-gods, sun- and cloud-gods, no more Time, just a bright eternal Now, my wife yawns, "That's enough already, let's go home, I did three autopsies today, I'd like a dish of Ben and Jerry's vanilla ice cream and a cup of decaf," houses on hills here and there, at the ends of fields, swamps and hilltops, ancient glacial landscapes, the house she didn't want to buy on the river ("I hate bridge-loans, I'm tired of moving"), no more walks at night ("I've been on my feet all day"), I get a letter from my old (72) widowed girlfriend in San Diego, "I'm on some sort of plateau now, I don't know how long I'll be here, but I wish you were here with me," the endless drives we used to take along the coast, up to Big Bear Lake, out to the desert, never enough, "I always feel like we're driving into God."

Seeing It

Not seeing it that differently since Dr. Marcus gave me my short-life sentence (metastases) last month, although going to a Christmas concert (Jew or not, what's the difference) at the Methodist church downtown, all the office buildings and restaurants (like ZOOP [soup with lots of garlic, exotic cheeses zest]), past the state capitol building, all sorts of memories begin to surface from my deep-sea depths, similar streets in Brooklyn, L.A., Berkeley, Philadelphia, Chicago, Buenos Aires, all my restaurant and zesty babe dates, all the blossoming Debussy and Schumann pianos and tubas, if only I could call my never-got-along-with Mom or made-out-of marble Dad, the old babe-friends, too-long-dead pals like Bukowski and Jorge Luis Borges, Neruda, memories almost becoming incarnate, in-stone, in-brick, want there to be an infinity of
                      forewords
                      that never
                      end,
                      end,
                      end.

Hugh Fox

Last Visit

They say it's his last few days, but they've been saying that for years, and he just (Elderly Care) keeps bumpin'-humpin' along, ninety-three, Mother Maria dead for ten years now, but ... I visit him every Friday afternoon, a little time off from my pathology lab, there he is waiting for me in the lounge, big place, a daughter visiting with her mother on the other end, and that's it, snow-warning outside, lake-effect, river-effect, pond-effect, how come I'm not in Brazil where my mother was from, "Hey, Sonny Boy, how ya doin'?," "OK," he stumbles to his feet and gives me the usual fatherly hug, hugging procedures he picked up from Brazilian-hugging Mom, "So I dreamt that I committed suicide last night, lots of leg pain, groin pain, they're talking about the cancer invading the bones now, more radiation, and sometimes I just want to end it, move from Painsville to Nowheresville, but ...," I'm curious, "What keeps you going?," "You, your sisters, the grandkids, I saw this film about Crabby Ass Beethoven last night, more than Crabby Ass, Mr. Incarnate Negativity, but at the most negative moment of his life he wrote his last symphony, you know, the choral one, which is heavenly ... and then I've been reading about Debussy and listening to him ... gotta keep the volume down in my room, they always keep complaining ... I just turn up my hearing aid ...," something I shouldn't ask, but ... "When you think about suicide, how do you think about doing it?," "Could be insecticides, a couple of shots in the brain, jumping into the Giselle River right now in the middle of winter, right through the ice ... a few minutes of agony, but ... Or maybe just leaving here some night and walking out into the forests, they're like endless ...," "Do you believe in afterlives?," hesitating, almost stuttering, getting up and walking round the

52

Primate Fox

couch for a minute, "Who knows, maybe this is my hundredth reincarnation, who knows, all those universes out there, dying and being born … maybe just believing creates it …," sitting back down, head bent down on his chest, a yawn, then getting up, "Siesta time …," another hug, "It's been great to see you," "Likewise," and I really mean it, a second hug, wave goodbye, back to the hospital, autopsies and endless slides, FNA's, when all I really ever wanted to be was a walrus or Christ tree, poodle, a river, the Amazon with eyes, flowing past endless, endless landscapes, down into endless seas.

Hugh Fox

ONCE AGAIN

First an orchiectomy, then transplants
and androgyn-estrogen pills that
start spring again, heat up the room and
pass the arthritis pain-killer, welcome
Diva Diane and Sculptured Kathleen
into my/our bedroom with the football-field-
sized bed that doesn't want touchdowns as
           much as
           touch (eternal)
           ups.

Cherimoya

Black seeds, seeds, seeds, each one wrapped in an off-white
sweet-as-possible fiber flesh, talking to me in the altiplano
Andes "We love snow … from a distance," like me, my Bolivian
wife making cherimoya juice every night, not quite oranges,
pears, cantaloupe, speaking Quechua as I chew it to death,
"*Machu Runa! Wiñas!* / Old Man! Forever!," which is fine
with me, remembering my hundred-and-five-year-old grandfather-
in-law, my hundred-and-twenty-year-old grandmother-in-law in
Tiawanaku, my wife always telling me "It cures cancer … why should
I lose you, you lose me …," finally coming to the point that I don't
    want anything else but sweet-chew eternity.

Hugh Fox

Wipe Up

So he's thirty and he still lives downstairs, works at a local Younker's, in charge of the Home Department, the jeans and Shag shirts gone, so his new girlfriend has four kids and doesn't work, but he's known her for ten years, got back together with her after his lawyer girlfriend told him to go hang himself, but not mention her name on his suicide farewell-note, money going out fast these days, thinking about buying his/their own house, marrying Jessica, my wife, his stepmom starting to resent everything about him, asking for ten dollars for gas when he borrows her car to go to work, when we go shopping together every Sunday after Chinese-buffet lunch, always buying a new shirt, another pair of jeans, baby clothes, who knows, an umbrella, boots for Jessica or Miriam, Jessica's latest baby, "He's a thief, I think he's on drugs, he's always borrowing old DVD films of yours, I bet he's selling them, and why didn't he get a girl with a degree, money, something up …," hate-spill instead of the usual (first thirty years) love-spill, at first I just endure it all, but then it begins to soak me in its acidic bitterness, HCl-vinegar, which I don't need at eighty, retired, soft sofas, loving that film about Stravinsky and Coco Chanel, another year or two before the cancer finally buries me, can't we just wipe it all up and spring comes, the mysteries start blooming, why not let them bloom in a wiped-up, rebirthing world?

Mid

Mid-bang on the wrong (formerly right) streets,
and you never know where these days, all my
old almost-RIP buddies still out/in there doing
their antique survival things, the invader kings
gone but still the snoots versus the inside-outers
wanting their own palace hills no matter who has
to be buried under them.

Hugh Fox

Listening

For the first time listening
to the poet voices
cawing-chirruping at me
through the winter
white-lace snow-skies,
"Neanderthal it back to
Sky-star-wind-rain
divinizing everything,
Mother mooning it
and Father sunning it,
deathlessly enclosed
in the omnipresent
faces and voices
that plug into the right
chemical visions that
swing back and forth
between—as if there were
a difference—dream-
reality or reality-dreams.

Time To …

Last night during the
almost cyclonic flurrying He
woke me up,
Him and his wind-whisper
meditating, "I think maybe
I'll start it
all over again, at least the
Earth-Ball … maybe no teeth
or nails,
LSD serenity built in, no
possibilities of
conquistadores, civil,
martial wars, maybe no
death, just x-number of
forever-evers,
a literate only vis-à-vis my
skies and whys, and maybe
I'll come back,
nail-less, cross-less
redemption, maybe
invisible, just an air-
presence,
no hair-presence, disinvent
heavens and hells, pass the
marzipan and let's *Concierto
de Aranjuez* it full time, one
language or who needs to talk,
one color, or who needs color
at all, walking forests once in a

Hugh Fox

while a storm, but never more
than just a little caressing
TO BE, TO BE, TO
BE

My Last Waltz

Should I Luschei them into carefully literary-ized ("Moon
sliver, you get rid of Al Power, desert extinction,
why nineteenth century such short lives") fragments,
give it to them the way it is, Bachianas Brasileiras-ing
again tonight, how come Alex mixes onions with guava
and uncooked beets, give it to me straight, how many
more hours, days, weeks do I have left, here I am next
to my Brazilian MD wife who makes $210,000 a year
and is my Czech grandma sweet, always one more or less
blanket, "A little honey on those cornflakes," from the
honey-farm down the road, all three wives hanging around
watching me die, e-mail (Lyn Strongin) XOXOs every
day from Vancouver, B.C., more Carpinteria, Tampa,
Rome, Santa Catarina ancient babes, two more novels
coming out this month, on the edge of Steinbeck/
Shakespeare, you wanna hear about the German
solid honey with my oat squares and a hundred before-
sleep hugs, or always another oncological-urological
smile?

Hugh Fox

SLIDING

Sliding through *Nova Rada Stala**
time, King Tut Hittite fear or let's
annihilate the Cherokees, Trojans,
Mayas, Ukrainians, Czechs, Shiites,
Pearl Harborians, Detroitists, Yankees …
searching for one patch of uncrucified
hallelujah corn-, wheat-, pig-, chicken-
land where grizzly machos/machas
have allowed a lifetime of blankets
and dumplings, potty-trainings,
eucharists and almond butter first
and last grades, the beards and baldness,
canes and chicken livers, as I lay me
down in peace (not pieces).

---

*   *Nova rada stala* – A New Joy. A Ukrainian Christmas song.

Fragmentos

1.

'Listen, I might as well tell you straight,' said Dr. Goldmark, 78, vastly overweight, his skin the color of old (sun-tan lotion/sun-lamp, or was it just him?) gold, always sounding like he was enunciating a papal decree about the Last Judgment/Armageddon, 'we've all gotta go. I've got prostate cancer myself, chemo-this, radiation-that, whatever I can do, but even without it I'd still have to go relatively soon, and …' 'Is that giving it to me straight or is it labyrinthically?'
John Bonnet in bed, as pale as whipped cream but still radiating out an aura of superman-ness, like he wasn't flesh and blood at all but some sort of cybernetic game figure.' 'So we're all doing to die, but that's not really what's on my mind.' 'I appreciate your making a house call,' a little weaker now, his Knight Templar psychological shield down.
'Well, we're pals and, you know, house calls were standard in the old days, my father made them all the time,' head down, a moment of prayer-homage, 'May he rest in peace.' 'Not me! Rest in turbulence!,' laughing, but Dr. Goldmark not responding, sitting there as serious as an empty picture frame on a living room wall.
'Why so serious? Is my end so imminent?' 'Look,' Goldmark persisting in almost solemnity, 'I've been reading your *fragmentos* for decades. There must be about fifteen volumes of them published by now.' 'Twenty-three. You don't have the early ones.' 'But I'd like to … how to put it … I'm serums and shots and x-rays, not thesauruses, and in all your work I feel messages, but they're always implicit, never quite spelled out,

no credos or papal declarations ... just for fun could you spell them out a little clearer for me.' 'Deathbed confession.' 'Lifebed confession.' 'I'm not any prophet or pope ... I've always declared, in fact, that I'm pure entertainment, no *messages*.' 'I wish I had a camera, a recorder...at least I have my...somewhat failing...memory.'
Bonnet suddenly getting very grim, preoccupied, squirming for a moment and then getting statue-fied. Goldmark had never seen him this way before, kept thinking Shakespeare, Julius Caesar, To Be or Not To Be, This is the Question, then Bonnet suddenly "lifting up," back against the bed, like he was ready to take

2.

the oath, 'Do you promise to tell the truth, the whole truth and ...' 'OK,' blinking, a little unsure and hesitant now, but still encyclical-ish, 'Let me give it a try....' Closing his eyes for a moment, Goldmark thinking he'd conked out, or worse, but then the words started in, like sleep-talking, soft, tiny-pawed, but at the same time in their own way Moses on the Mount prophetic, 'First of all, no Amorites versus the ancient Jews' nonsense, with God on the Jews' side: 'You can kill them and their children, take their animals and land.' I and Thou became US, no matter what the beliefs, languages, colors, all part of the same club. To be human is to be same human, in fact glorying in differences. And it's true, the whole time I was growing up in Portland, the more foreign/exotic the better, my parents

Primate Fox

liked diversity like it was precious gems, that was the main thing, *abraços*, nothing to do with murder. Like sometimes I go into these fancy chain-restaurants and over in the corner there's this whole family, a birthday party or something, all the grandmas and grandpas, kids, grand-kids, great-grand-kids … or maybe it's a few old women together, I always think widows, sometimes a few survivor guys … you get the sense of like there's something inside them all that says 'This is great, the way it ought to be,' I know it sounds corny, but I don't even want to say love, let's call it one tribe, the whole world as one tribe, you see another colored face, hear another language, and instead of turning you off, it turns you on. I'm an ex-Catholic-turned-Jew, maybe I want Christmas back, the Savior coming and he comes, we're saved, in our synagogue the local Moslem minister comes and gives sermons, we go over to the mosque, the Rabbi talks there. Love black, love YAKSA MASH, DOBCHA, Polish-Czech … love Oriental, everyone works, not just a few big shots on top and everyone losing their jobs and houses, everything imported, nothing made here, build new furniture factories, grow cotton, weave wool, make shoes and carpets, radiators and screwdrivers, hair-dryers … and re-create neighborhoods, parks, a sense of belonging, turn off the imports and limit lap-top time … I'm back on the river and in the Scottish Highlands, on the seaside, in Cádiz, Spain, in Venice and Stockholm, pass the dumplings in Prague and then come back to the working woman-man USA … and the wild turkeys keep turkeying through my head, the deer and grouse… even in the middle of the city, like in Cambridge.…'

He stops, worn out, there's obviously a lot more to share/say, but he's not up to it.

'So, OK,' says Goldmark, 'Any major problems or changes and give me a call, there's that Mrs. Gorman who lives upstairs, right? Free room and board for a little now-and-then care.' 'I've got an emergency bell if I need her,' pointing to a little bell-

3.

pad on the table next to the bed, 'she's a good cook, lots of corned beef and cabbage. As Irish as I was supposed to be growing up …' 'We should have all stayed 'there,' you know what I mean, our pasts. Me in a *shtetl* in Bohemia somewhere, you in Athenry, no Nazis, no potato famines,' stopping, looking up at and then beyond the ceiling, a look of hope turning slowly to disgruntlement, then a final smile and 'Shalom,' and he was gone and Bonnet closed his eyes and let the rains of exhaustion washed him painlessly into dreamless sleep.

Rebirthing Without Having To Die

"Stare into the candles, forget the 'miracles' of the lights,"
she says, and we all stare, stare, stare, half an hour, all the
time her whispering, "stare at the steppes, the peaks, the
v-formation ducks and geese, the grasses and the flowers,
at yourself in the mirror, at your family-faces, stare, listen to
the wind, the friends on the phone, over coffee, listen to the river,
touch, hands, body, touch, touch, breathe, BE no after-
anything, but now-everything … the sky at night, up in
the Himalayas at midnight, billions of other Nows out
there staring back at you …," finally the candles finishing
up, no one moving for a few minutes, and when they do
move, suddenly all the faces, eyes, fragrances, their clothes
      on their bodies, their feet in their shoes,
           THERE.

Hugh Fox

Getting Confused

Between Westminster Abbey and Oxford, wives one
and three, granddaughters Rebecca and Gabrielle,
the year, month, season, the moon brooding over the forty-
five degree July night as Chris (19) tells me Clarice just had
her period, she's not pregnant, but Jessica's coming back from
California with his six-month-old daughter inside her, "Should
I be a film director, actor, porn star, insurance man, computer
nerd or just go on disability like my mother (wife number 2)
or my sister, Cecilia? "Look at those houses on the ledges," I
answer him, "What a view of the river a hundred feet below,
although I suppose the whole thing could give way with the
slightest tremor and you'd end up buried under twenty tons
of rock," twenty tons or a few feet, an Indian jet goes down and
Bernadette says, "That could be us if we had gone to Brazil,"
only we didn't go to Brazil, we went to Cleveland instead.

Survival

Sun-Dance survival, in teepee-touch
with the feather-arrow realities of
real Inca-Maya-Sioux-Dakota
America, plugged into the sun-star
rhythms of survival-reality, the
Englishers and Spanishers and
Portuguesers spreading out to
erase histories that still fragment
into everyday-ness even in
bytesville reality.

Hugh Fox

BACK AGAIN

Maybe it was too much biochemistry and oncology, cynicism, deaths,
after the from-Ireland nuns and brothers, daily Mass and Communion,
walking out into agnostic keep-going-anyhow-ness until my mind started
re-looking at gall bladders and life-seeds falling into uterine fields,
another and another and another birth, surrounded by my own births and
a year up in the Atacama Desert in Chile where I could read a newspaper
by million-strong starlight, however, whoever, rain-snow storms of
impossibles never leaving me alone until the cancer came back and
suddenly the Bleed-Mes came back again, just before almost-sleep,
during the miracle sun, trees, grouse, cranes, toenails, Notre Dame,
                                miracle twenty-fours.

Turning Off

Turning off all the cyber-electro-heaven everythings,
up into the Chilean Andes where at night you
can read *Purgatorio*, or let's try the year-turn
center at Tiawanaku, slide down to Lourdes'
house on Santa Catarina, where floating
is like floating in your own blood,
you can even find those middle-of-everything/
nothing Michigan, New Hampshire, Massachusetts
wild forest-farm areas where someone-God is
humming full-time, what eyes, skin, ears are
                really made for.

Hugh Fox

Pavanes

Pavanes for a hundred years back mornings
when my grandmother gave birth to my mother
and the afternoon baby George died, crushed
by a tree in a Tennessee tornado, for Bernadette's
aging eyes and fumbling fingers, shaking at times
like an elm on October 31st, for Mozart,
Schumann, Lili Boulanger, Debussy and Coco
Chanel, for the billion years I won't be here,
all the streets and faces, races, graces, capitals,
cars, bars, that ... you tell me!

Zenning

Zenning into the core
of every moment,
moment by moment,
hour by year, year by decade,
seeing *Amazonas*
water lily pads,
huge water buffalos
and a naked black African-Brazilian
girl, the Urubamba River,
vultures eating
fish-guts, wharves at Belén
my wife's face going from 20
to 80 in as long as it takes
to write these lines.

Hugh Fox

La Paix

Musée Marc-Aurèle Fortin

La paix, la paix,
la paix, je suis
Musulman-Juif,
Chretienne-Athée
comme vous voulez, mais
quel importe, les arbres,
le ciel, un peu de satiété dans
l'air, les saisons changent,
les jambes, les seins, les visages,
tout devient archaeologique,
les os dans les tombes,
les maisons en ruines,
les toits, les vieux moulins,
la paix
qui sourit.

PEACE

> Musée Marc-Aurèle Fortin

Peace, peace,
peace, I'm
Muslim -Jew,
Christian-Atheist,
whatever you want,
but what's the difference, the trees,
the sky, a little fullness in
the air, the seasons change,
the legs, the breasts, the faces,
everything becomes archaeological,
bones in tombs,
the houses in ruins,
the roofs, the old mills,
smiling peace
remains.

Hugh Fox

Brusquement

Brusquement toute devient
les cheveux au vent,
les nouvelles feuilles,
notre peau,
un moment blanc,
le prochain noir,
jaune,
les théologies d'antiquité (presque)
(mais vraiment pas si antique)
abandonnés pour modeler
notre propre théologie faite
desdéesses , nous dans
l'univers
fait de notre peau et os.

Suddenly

Suddenly everything becomes
hair in the wind,
the new leaves,
our skin,
one moment white,
the next black,
yellow, escaping
the theologies of antiquity (almost)
(but not really that antique)
to form our own theology made
out of goddesses, ourselves in the
universe
made out of
our own skin
and bones.

Acknowledgements

Grateful acknowledgement is made to the editors of the following publications, where versions of these poems originally appeared:

Presa: "Re-Inspiriting"
Medulla Review: "Blu-Ray Rerun"
Anastomoo: "Back Home"
Front Porch Review: "The Time Of"
Viral Cat Press: "In Between"
Sketchbook: "Re-In-Psyche-Action"
Magma (UK): "Primate Fox"
Hinchas de Poesia: "To Look / Olhar"
Haggard and Halloo: "Christmas(ing)," "All of a Sudden"
Toucan: "Iguatemi"
The Centrifugal Eye: "Loving"
The Neglected Ratio: "Alternatives," "From Now," "Now," "The Insider Me"
Avatar: "The Eternal"
Blue Stem Magazine: "Wherevers"
House Organ: "Class War"
The Beatnik: "What Do I?"
The Flea: "Since"
Slipstream: "Death-Sentence"
Morphrog: "Re-dying," "Walking Into," "Going Back," "Turning Into"
vis a tergo: "The Seconds"
Lyrical Somerville, a section of the *Somerville News:* "Everyday Shalom"
The Montreal Review: "Versus," "Getting Inside," "Turning," "Every"

Vox Poetica: "The Closer," "Words," "The Confessional Diary of Bone Boning"
The Laurel Review: "Toy Storing"
River Oak Review: "Our Afternoon Drive"
Hamilton Stone Review: "Seeing It"
The Monongahela Review: "Last Visit"
Bluestem: "Once Again"
Umbrella Factory Magazine: "Cherimoya"
The Inkblot: "Wipe Up"
Midwestern Gothic: "Mid"
Cyclamens and Swords Publishing: "Listening," "Everything," "Time To …"
Split: "Wipe Up"
Semolina Pilchard: "My Last Waltz"
Jellyroll Magazine: "Sliding," "Rebirthing Without Having to Die"
Main Street Rag: "Getting Confused," "Survival"
Dappled Things: "Back Again"
New Letters: "Turning Off," "Pavanes"
Mad Hatters' Review: "Zenning," "*La Paix* / Peace," "*Brusquement* / Suddenly," "*Fragmentos*"

HUGH BERNARD FOX JR. (1932 – 2011), born in Chicago, was a writer, novelist, poet and anthropologist and one of the founders (with Ralph Ellison, Anaïs Nin, Paul Bowles, Joyce Carol Oates, Reynolds Price and others) of the Pushcart Prize for literature. He received a Ph.D. in American Literature from the University of Illinois at Urbana-Champaign, and was a professor at Michigan State University in the Department of American Thought and Language from 1968 until his retirement in 1999.

He received Fulbright Professsorships at the University of Hermosillo in Mexico in 1961, the Instituto Pedagogico and Universidad Catlica in Caracas from 1964 to 1966, and at the University of Santa Catarina in Brazil from 1978-1980. He met his third wife Maria Bernadete Costa in Brazil in 1978. He studied Latin American literature at the University of Buenos Aires, received an OAS grant and spent a year as an archaeologist in the Atacama Desert in Chile in 1986. He was the founder and Board of Directors member of COSMEP, the International Organization of Independent Publishers, from 1968 until its death in 1996. He was editor of *Ghost Dance: The International Quarterly of Experimental Poetry* from 1968-1995.

He wrote over fifty-four books of poetry, many volumes of short fiction and novels. Hugh's final novel was *Reunion*, published by Luminis Books in summer 2011. *Primate Fox* is Hugh's last collection of poems.

www.ingramcontent.com/pod-product-compliance
Lightning Source LLC
Chambersburg PA
CBHW051702090426
42736CB00013B/2507